HITTIN' THE TRAIL: MINNESOTA

Day Hiking Trails of
Split Rock Lighthouse State Park

I0116056

By Rob Bignell

Atiswinic Press · Ojai, Calif.

DAY HIKING TRAILS OF SPLIT ROCK LIGHTHOUSE STATE PARK

A GUIDEBOOK IN THE
HITTIN' THE TRAIL: MINNESOTA SERIES

Copyright Rob Bignell, 2017

Atiswinic Press
Ojai, Calif. 93023
hikeswithtykes.com/hittinthetrail_home.html

ISBN 978-0-9961625-8-6

Cover design by Rob Bignell
Cover photo of Split Rock Lighthouse
All interior photos by Rob Bignell

Manufactured in the United States of America
First printing May 2017

Dedication

For Kieran

Contents

Introduction

I magine a place where you can hike the grounds of a historic lighthouse that for decades kept ships safe from jagged, killer rocks; where trails offer fantastic vistas of the world's largest freshwater lake and take you along quaint pebble and cobblestone beaches; where easy walks pass strange geological formations formed in the violent rending of a continent more than a billion years ago; where paths cross through the remnants of a pioneer-era logging camp and a turn-of-the century mining operation. The place is real: It's called Split Rock Lighthouse State Park.

Located along Minnesota's North Shore a little more than 45 miles northeast of Duluth, Split Rock state park is an outdoor recreational paradise, as well as a site of historical importance. Among Minnesota's most visited state parks, it's popular with hikers, campers and nature lovers of all stripes, garnering about 340,000 annual visitors.

Geology

Split Rock's great scenery would not exist but for 1.1 billion-year-old lava flows that formed when North America began to separate into two, creating what today is called the Mid-Continent Rift. The rift extends all across the Great Lakes to as far south as Kansas.

In Minnesota, those lava flows along Lake Superior are known as the North Shore Volcanic Group. Occurring over millions of years, the flows can run up to 30,000 feet.

Much of the state park sits atop a single, large block of

anorthosite. A buoyant mineral, it floated atop the magma as the rift grew. The mineral is also quite resistant to erosion – so resistant that during the early 1900s the Minnesota Mining and Manufacturing Company (now known as 3M) mistakenly thought the North Shore rock might by corundum, which is used in abrasives.

Fast forward to 10,000 B.C. The great glaciers of the last ice age have scraped off eons of accumulated sediment, leaving only the basalt and a thin layer of till over them. Cold Lake Superior is merely what remains of a melted glacier in a low spot of the 1.1 billion-year-old rift. Rivers all along the North Shore are carving through the remaining till and sediment and exposing the underlying basalt.

Geography

Several day hiking trails explore Split Rock state park's fascinating geography. The park essentially consists of two landscapes.

The first is the highlands that rise a few hundred feet above Lake Superior. This entire section is located west of Minn. Hwy. 61. The **Split Rock River Trail** runs alongside Split Rock River as the waterway cuts downward through the highlands toward Lake Superior. The **Merrill Logging Trail** follows a former rail line that winds into the highlands. The **Superior Hiking Trail** runs the highlands' length.

The rocky shoreline with several headlands – erosion-resistant rock that sticks out into the lake – forms the second geographical region. All of it is east of Hwy. 61. Among the headlands, from north to south, are Split Rock Point, Corundum Point (which includes Day Hill), Stony Point (where the lighthouse is located), and Gold Rock Point.

Stony Point, which rises about 150 feet straight out of the lake, is the most dramatic of the park's vistas. The **Split Rock Light Station Trail** runs across the top of Stony Point while the **Little Two Harbors Trail** heads down that point to a rocky shoreline on a cove.

History

Minnesota's Split Rock Lighthouse State Park enjoys a rich history that ranges from shipping and mining to Native Americans and modern tourism. Several of the park's day hiking trails explore this past.

Ojibwa Indians dominated the entire Minnesota North shore beginning in the 1700s. By the mid-1800s, the first white settlers in what is now the state park established a fishing village at Little Two Harbors. Cement foundations of the houses and fish processing buildings are all that remain.

From 1899-1906, a logging camp was set up at the mouth of the Split Rock River, down shore from Little Two Harbors. A rail line heading into the highlands also was constructed.

In 1901, the North Shore Abrasives Company set up shop at Corundum Point after a prospector misidentified the anorthosite there as corundum, which is used as an industrial abrasive. When the company realized it had the wrong rock, operations were abandoned. Cement footings of the company's building and other relics from the mining operation still can be found at the park.

A horrible gale in November 1905 damaged 29 of U.S. Steel's bulk ore carriers on Lake Superior. Two of them were wrecked on the rocky shoreline that now is the state park. The result was construction of Split Rock Lighthouse, which is the park's main attraction. It became operational in 1910.

After Hwy. 61 was constructed in 1924, the lighthouse became an unintentional tourist attraction. Thousands of people began parking on the road and walking through the woods to the scenic point where the lighthouse stood.

A half century later, however, technology had made the old lighthouses obsolete. Many lighthouses across the country subsequently were automated while others closed. In 1969, Split Rock's lighthouse was shut down.

Two years later, the state of Minnesota purchased the 25-acre lighthouse site. It was restored to its early 1920s appearance. Today, the lighthouse ranks among Minnesota's 10 most-visited state park.

When to Visit

The best months to day hike Split Rock Lighthouse State Park and nearby trails are mid-May through September. Depending on the year, April and October also can be pleasant.

During spring, waterfalls run at their highest levels, the bird migration is in full swing, and bugs are nil. Trails can be muddy, though, as snow typically melts between April and early May.

Unlike the rest of Minnesota, summers at Split Rock usually are not humid, as cool breezes off Lake Superior keep heat and most insects at bay. Rain, however, can occur during the afternoon even when the morning is sunny, so always check the weather forecast before heading out.

For many hikers, autumn marks the best time to hit a Split Rock trail. By mid-August, summer's few bugs are gone, trails mostly are dry, and throughout September maples and aspen light the wilderness with color. A sweatshirt often is needed during the day, though, and nights can be chilly.

Mid-October through March usually is too cold and wet for day hiking. Once snow falls, trails typically are used for cross-country skiing, snowmobiling or snowshoeing.

How to Get There

Several major highways offer access to Split Rock. All converge in Duluth, and from there, it's roughly 25 miles north via Minn. Hwy. 61 to Two Harbors and then another 20 miles north to the state park.

From the Minneapolis-St. Paul area, take Interstate 35 to Duluth. When I-35 ends, the road becomes Hwy. 61. If in northern Minnesota, take either U.S. Hwy. 2 or U.S. Hwy 53 to Duluth.

If in northern or eastern Wisconsin, U.S. Hwys. 45 and 51 as well as Wis. Hwy. 13 all lead to Hwy. 2, which travels west to Duluth. From western Wisconsin, U.S. Hwy. 63 as well as Wis. Hwy. 35 both head north head to Hwy. 2. Hwy. 53 runs from Interstate 94 at Eau Claire into Duluth; it's the only combination of four-lane highways connecting most of Wisconsin to Duluth.

From Canada, in Thunder Bay take Hwy. 61 south to the United States border. The road becomes Minn. Hwy. 61 once in the States and leads directly to Split Rock.

Maps

To properly prepare for any hike, you should examine maps before hitting the trail and bring them with you (See the Bonus Section for more.). No guidebook can reproduce a map as well as the satellite pictures or topographical maps that you can find online for free. To that end, a companion website to this book offers printable maps for each featured trail at *dayhikingtrails.wordpress.com/trail-maps*.

Split Rock Lighthouse State Park

T hough incredibly diverse in its trail offerings, Split Rock Lighthouse State Park is not so large that they can't all be hiked in a week. Many visitors to the North Shore usually tackle one or two of them a visit over several years. Whichever approach you use, each day hike is certain to lead to a wonderful experience and memory.

Split Rock River Trail

A red rock gorge with waterfalls awaits on the Split Rock River Trail.

Due to the great scenery and ease of access, the 4.4-miles round trip trail is among the Superior Hiking Trail's most popular segments. To reach the trail, from Two Harbors, drive north on Minn. Hwy. 61. At mile marker 43.2, turn into the parking lot for the Split River Rock DOT Wayside on the road's north side.

The path heads up the west shore of Split Rock River through a birch grove on a spur trail. The spur is a gradual climb, offering scenic views of the river valley below. Be aware that the clay banks on this side of the root beer-colored river at times are steep and after a rainfall can be slick; boardwalks, timbers and bridges make up part of the rugged trail's surface.

At 0.5 miles from the trailhead, the spur reaches the junction with the actual Superior Hiking Trail; go right/north, remaining along the river. Watch for the blue blazes that mark the SHT.

A wooden bridge crosses the West Fork of the Split River, a small creek that drains into the main waterway, at about 0.8 miles from the trailhead. Large, mature cedars grow near the confluence, and a rock ledge allows a great place to rest and even enjoy a picnic as viewing Split Rock Falls, which tumbles 20 feet over gray rock.

From the creek, the trail swerves back to the river and enters a magnificent red rock gorge. The rock is rhyolite, a form of granite that appears red though its crystals are pink, black and white

It formed during a massive lava flow 1.1 billion years ago.

A bare, shear five-story cliff of rhyolite is visible on the opposite shore. The green conifers atop this wall nicely contrast with the red rock.

Cascades and a small waterfall also can be found within the gorge.

Also among the highlights is the Pillars, twin chimneys of rhyolite. They sometimes are referred to as "Split Rock," though that appellation probably came after the park was named. Passing the formation, look back as the pillars frame the waterfalls in the gorge.

Leaving the gorge, the trail levels out. At 2.4 miles, it reaches a footbridge over the Split River; this marks a good spot to turn back to the parking lot.

Additional hike

If you have a little extra energy, consider making a loop around the river. Rather than turn back at the bridge, cross it to the river's east side for a 5-mile round trip.

This trail on the eastern/northern shoreline is higher, staying above the gorge. Combined with the greater amount

Split Rock River Trail

of sunlight the slopes on this side of the river receive, this is a drier portion of the trail. The cliffs also offer a unique vantage for seeing the Pillars.

The trail soon moves away from the river and climbs a bit higher to a ridgeline. The result is a wide, commanding view of Lake Superior with the Apostle Islands in the distance. A lean-to shelter is near this vista.

At 4.2 miles from the parking lot, the Superior Hiking Trail comes to a junction; take the spur trail right/southeast. The trail then makes a steep descent. At the bottom, you'll cross Hwy. 61. From there, go left, southwest on the paved Gitchi-Gami State Trail.

The trail then crosses Split Rock as it spills into Lake Superior. Use the pedestrian tunnel to cross Hwy. 61 to your parking lot.

Gitchi-Gami State Trail

Day hikers can get a good sense of what Split Rock Lighthouse State Park is all about via the Gitchi-Gami State Trail, the only route that runs from one end of the park to the other.

Though primarily a bicycle trail, the paved Gitchi-Gami can be walked as well. When completed, the trail will run 88-miles from Two Harbors to Grand Marais. One of its longest finished sections runs from Gooseberry Falls State Park to Beaver Bay, which takes it straight through Split Rock.

The trail rambles about 3.8 miles across the park. If split up, three trail segments make for great day hikes.

DOT Wayside to Park Road segment

This 2.6-mile (one-way) section cuts across Split Rock's southern half.

To reach the trailhead, from Two Harbors take Minn. Hwy. 61 about 21 miles north. At Split Rock Lighthouse State Park, park at the DOT wayside overlooking Split Rock River.

From the wayside, pick up the stem trail on the lot's west side, taking it under the highway to the trail, which runs between the highway and Lake Superior. There's a small sand bar beyond the stem and the main trail's intersection. A logging camp existed here in 1899-1906.

Go left/northeast on the main trail and cross the Split Rock River's mouth with Lake Superior. In short order, you'll reach the junction with the Corundum Mine Trail. That trail explores the remnants of a mining operation from the early 1900s.

At 0.3 miles from the trailhead, the Gitchi-Gami junctions with the Merrill Logging Trail. The Merrill Logging Trail was built on an old railroad grade that brought white pine from the Arrowhead to Lake Superior.

In 0.9 miles from the trailhead, you'll come across the jun-

Gitchi-Gami State Trail near DOT wayside

ction with a connector trail that heads to the Corundum Mine Trail. At 1.2 miles is the junction with the other end of Corundum Mine Trail.

The Gitchi-Gami next crosses Rock Creek, which flows out of the highlands into Lake Superior.

On the other side of bridge is a connector leading to the Day Hill Trail. At 1.4 miles, you'll come to yet another connector to that trail. Day Hill is a large block of erosion-resistant anorthosite that is more than a billion years old.

At 1.5 miles, the Gitchi-Gami reaches a three-way intersection with the Day Hill Trail. Go left/north and hike the backside of Day Hill and its base as you come back alongside Hwy. 61.

Along the way, you'll a pass wayside for Hwy. 61. From the wayside, you'll get an outstanding view of the Split Rock Lighthouse, which was constructed on 1910.

At 2.6 miles, the Gitchi-Gami reaches the park road.

Though you've hardly covered the length of the trail in Split Rock, this marks a good spot to turn back for a 5.2-mile round trip.

Split Rock light station to Park Road segment

This 0.6-miles one-way hike (1.2-miles round trip) runs through the park's center portion.

To reach the trailhead, enter Split Rock as if going to the light station and park in its lots. From the southwest lot, pick up the access trail. When the trail splits, go left/south-west.

The trail follows the park road then swerves away from it to near the Little Two Harbors Trail. The Little Two Har-bors offers great views of Lake Superior and leads to a beach.

Next the Gitchi-Gami crosses a creek. When it arrives at the park road, you've reached the spot where the previous segment ended. This marks a good spot to turn back.

Split Rock light station to Gold Rock Point segment

This 0.9-mile one-way (1.8-mile round trip) heads into park's northern section.

Enter the park as if going to the Split Rock light station and park in its lots. As in the previous segment, from the southwest lot, pick up the access trail. When the trail splits, however, go right/north-east and cross the park road.

The trail closely parallels the park road then Hwy. 61 for 0.8 miles, where it arrives at a parking lot. From the lot, a 0.1-mile spur trail heads to a bay west of Gold Rock Point.

On the point, you can look for agates and try to spot in the shallow water the remains of the cargo ship *Madeira*, which sunk here in 1905.

On Nov. 28 of that year, a fierce storm with winds of up to 80 mph hit the area. Unable to handle the swells, the schoon-er smashed into the Gold Rock cliff. One crewman was able to leap ashore and with a safety line help eight others off, only to watch their ship sink and remain stranded for two days on the cliffside.

After taking in the lake views, retrace yours steps back to the lot. Alternately, you can continue north/east from parking lot to park boundary, which is in 0.7 miles; that addition, which crosses two creeks, makes for a 3.2-mile round trip hike.

Final note: Though the trail runs through wooded areas its entire length in Split Rock, it is wide, so you'll want to wear a sunhat and don sunscreen.

Corundum Mine Trail

Day hikers can explore the history of a wild Lake Superior shoreline on the Corundum Mine Trail.

The route runs 4.2-miles round trip. Besides being a back-to-nature hike, the trail passes ruins of old logging and mining operations.

To reach the trailhead, take Minn. Hwy. 61 about 21 miles north from Two Harbors. At Split Rock Lighthouse State Park, park at the DOT wayside overlooking Split Rock River.

From the wayside, pick up the stem trail on the lot's west side, taking it under the highway to the paved Gitchi-Gami State Trail, which runs between the highway and Lake Superior.

There's a small sand bar beyond the stem and the main trail's intersection.

Go left/northeast on the main trail and cross the Split Rock River's mouth with Lake Superior. Keep an eye out for the remains of pilings, a wharf, and a dam that once was part of the Split Rock Lumber Company's logging operations from 1899 to 1906.

At 0.2 miles from the parking lot, you'll reach the actual Corundum Mine Trail. Go right/southeast onto the path, as it edges a forested side of Split Rock Point. A post office and other buildings where the lumberjacks resided used to sit inland on the point.

The trail reaches an impressive overlook of Lake Superior at 0.7 miles from the wayside. A young lake, Superior formed when a massive glacier during the last ice age scooped out the soft sediment and then melted in the massive depression.

From the overlook, the trail cuts inland than passes Crazy Bay. A small cobblestone beach separates the woods from the lake, where seagulls soar overhead as Corundum Point rises out of the northeast. It's a great location for a picnic lunch. The spot is popular with kayakers, and there's a campsite for them at 1.2 miles from the trailhead.

The trail remains close to the lakeshore the rest of the way. At 1.5 miles from the trailhead, it reaches a connecting trail with the Gitchi-Gami; continue going straight/northeast.

A knoll soon appears on the horizon. This is the peak on Corundum Point. At the 2-mile mark, the trail reaches the knoll's base. Despite that glaciers have covered the point several times, the highly-resistant anorthosite rock survived.

The two large concrete footings along the trail are the remains of a crushing house built more than a century ago by the North Shore Abrasives Company. Many mistook the anorthosite for corundum, the hardest mineral after diamonds.

A steep 0.1-mile spur trail heads to an overlook atop the knoll. After taking in the view, retrace your steps back to the wayside parking lot.

Merrill Logging Trail

Day hikers can travel into the bluffs overlooking Lake Superior via a century-old railroad grade on this trail.

The Merrill Logging Trail, including an access trail from Split Rock River, runs 2.7-miles round trip. It crosses an area that many visiting the state rock bypass in favor of the historic lighthouse.

To reach the trailhead, from Two Harbors travel north on Minn. Hwy. 61. Park at the DOT Wayside for Split Rock River. From the lot, go north on the walking path and take an immediate left/north onto the access trail for the Gitchi-Gami State Trail; this stem runs under the highway.

Once at the main trail, go left/northeast onto it. Follow it for 0.25 miles, then turn left/north onto the Merrill Logging Trail. A crossing of Hwy. 61 is required here, so be careful, as the road is busy.

Once across the highway, the grassy trail angles to the northeast into the woodline and climbs the Merrill Grade. Though steep, gaining about 150 feet in 1.1 miles, it is the easiest way to head up the bluffside.

From 1899 to 1906, the Merrill & Ring Lumber Company ran a logging camp at the mouth of the Split Rock River. A rail line headed 10 miles into the bluffs and backcountry, hauling timber to the river mouth. The trail follows a segment of that rail line.

About 0.2 miles from the Gitchi-Gami, the Merrill route reaches its first trail junction, a connector to the Superior Hiking Trail. Continue straight/northeast.

During the 1860s, Thomas Merrill – the product of a Maine lumber family – started a number of logging companies in Michigan. In 1886, he joined forces with Clark Ring, and they based their company out of Saginaw, Mich.

In another 0.2 miles, the walking path junctions another connector to the Superior Hiking Trail. Go right/east here and continue up the bluff. In short order, the trail angles north.

As the white pine forests of the Great Lakes states thinned in the 1890s, Merrill & Ring purchased land in Washington state. In 1902, they moved their headquarters there.

About 0.7 miles from the last junction, the Merrill Logging

Trail intersects the Superior Hiking Trail at Split Rock Creek. The creek rises from even higher in the bluffs, at an elevation more than 200 feet above this point.

The creek marks the park's northern boundary and the end of the Merrill Logging Trail. Turn back here, retracing your steps back to the wayside parking lot.

Superior Hiking Trail, Southeast Split Rock River Campsite, ATV Trail on Chapins Ridge segments

Day hikers can enjoy great views of Lake Superior on two segments of the Superior Hiking Trail in the state park.

While the segments share the same access trails, upon reaching the SHT, hikers can go in one of two directions – left/southwest to the Southeast Split Rock River Campsite or right/northeast to an ATV trail on Chapins Ridge. The former is shorter while the latter offers better vistas of Lake Superior.

To reach the trailhead, from Two Harbors travel north on Minn. Hwy. 61. Park at the Split Rock River DOT Wayside. Take the access trail around the lot and under the highway to the Gitchi-Gami State Trail. Go left/northeast on the trail.

In 0.3 miles, look for the Merrill Logging Trail. It is to the left on the other side of Hwy. 61 and is marked with a yellow gate. Carefully cross the busy highway to the trail; you may need to walk a ways in the ditch or along the shoulder to reach the gate.

After walking 0.2 miles up a steep grade, you'll reach the first junction with a connector to the SHT. Go left/northwest onto in. These by far are the most arduous portions of the hike.

In 0.2 miles, you'll reach the SHT. You'll have to decide there which segment you want to take.

Left/southwest to Split Rock River campsite

This route heads to the Southeast Split Rock River Campsite for a 3.2-mile round trip from the DOT Wayside.

When the connector reaches the SHT, go left/southwest. For most of this segment, the trail follows the ridgeline at about 850 feet elevation. It's about 0.9 miles from the connector to the campsite.

The campsite marks a good spot to turn back. Alternately, you can continue on; in 0.6 miles is the footbridge across the Split Rock River. This reaches the end of the Split Rock Riv-er Trail described earlier in the book.

Right/northeast to ATV Trail

Following the ridgeline, the trail offers excellent vistas of Lake Superior and the Split Rock Lighthouse below for a 5.6-mile round trip.

When the connector and the SHT meet, go right/north-east.

Along the way, the trail passes several rock outcroppings. Most of these mark the former shoreline of ancient Glacial Lake Duluth.

The trail soon begins a long but gradual descent to a wetlands surrounding Split Rock Creek. A footbridge heads over the stream, and then it's uphill once more.

Next the SHT junctions with the Merrill Logging Trail at 0.8 miles from the connector. From there, the SHT leaves the state park, as heading north along the century-old railroad line that was used to haul fallen logs out of the highlands to the lake.

Eventually the SHT splits from the old railroad grade and heads through a spruce forest. Rocky ridges with steep drops and lichen-covered boulders offer visual delights.

In 1.3 miles from the Merrill Logging Trail, the SHT inter-sects an ATV trail. This marks a good spot to turn back. If continuing on, however, the SHT reaches the Chapins Ridge Campsite in 0.4 miles.

Split Rock Creek Trail

Day hikers can explore a bluffside overlooking Lake Superior on the Split Rock Creek Trail.

The 2.5-miles round trip trail parallels Split Rock Creek. It's one of the park's less hiked trails and so offers a nice dose of solitude.

To reach the trailhead, from Minn. Hwy. 61 use the park's main entry road for the historical lighthouse. Follow the road all the way to its end, where there's a parking lot.

The trail leaves from the lot's south side, heading to Lake Superior. Pass through the first junction then in 0.1 miles from the lot, at the second junction, go right/northwest on the Day Hill Trail. For the next 0.4 miles, the trail wraps around the hill's northern base.

Upon reaching the paved Gitchi-Gami State Trail, go left/ southwest for 0.15 miles. At the second intersection, go right /west; you're now on the Split Rock Creek Trail.

Juneberry bushes grow in abundance for the next 0.1 miles as the trail reaches Hwy. 61. Sometimes called service berries, Saskatoon or shadbush, the fruit looks very similar to blueberries but tastes more like black cherries. The fruit typically ripens in late June to early July.

Carefully cross the busy highway and continue up the slope paralleling Split Rock Creek past birch and alder trees for the next 0.5 miles. The trail climbs more than 100 feet during that stretch.

A wide jeep trail, the Split Rock is wooded the entire way. Most of the stretch consists of spruce and maple with a large number of birch and balsam poplar dead or dying. Beneath the birch, look for flat-topped white, large-leaf, and pinnacled asters. These plants are typical of aging birch forests along

Lake Superior.

Plants common in local grassy lawns have to be mowed in sections where they're taking over the trail. Among them are buttercups, plantain, red and white clover, strawberries. Meanwhile, bracken fern, bush honeysuckle, large-leafed aster, and raspberries line the trail as it ascends.

Geology-wise, the trail crosses an outcrop of diabase, a hard, erosion-resistant rock that has existed here for more than a billion years. A couple of the boulders in the outcrop that stand out consist of dark-colored schist and another of pink monzonite.

As gaining altitude, the trail pass white cedar with high branches. The lower branches all have been browsed by white-tailed deer. The region's large deer population is problematic for many trees, especially younger ones whose leaves are tastier.

One thing you won't see too much of is Split Rock Creek, which mostly is separated from the trail by trees. Forming farther up in the highlands, the creek spills into Lake Superior between Split Rock and Corundum points. Older maps do not list it Split Rock Creek – the stream actually has no official name – though locals have called it that since the 1920s, and most official Minnesota maps now refer to us as such.

After passing through a grove of large, aged cedars with younger, smaller balsam poplars, you're closing in on the Superior Hiking Trail. At the SHT, turn back, retracing your steps back to the parking lot.

Day Hill Trail

Hikers can head to what is arguably one of the North Shore's best vistas on the Day Hill Trail at the geographical center of the state park.

Two routes can take you to the top of this tall chunk of

volcanic rock that sits over Lake Superior. The shorter out-and-back trail runs about 1.4-miles round trip while a longer lollipop trail runs about 1.8 miles.

To reach the trailhead, from Two Harbors, drive north on Minn. Hwy. 61 for 19 miles. Use the park entrance road for the lighthouse but continue driving southwest to the parking lot at its end. The Day Hill Trail leaves from the lot's south side. At the first trail junction, continue straight/south.

Short route

At the next junction, go right/north. The well-groomed trail heads 0.4 miles around Day Hill's north side, gradually ascending the rock. Day Hill is a large block of anorthosite, one of three in the park, the other two being Corundum Point and Stony Point. Formed 1.1 billion years ago, anorthosite lacks iron-bearing minerals so is highly resistant to erosion.

At the next junction, turn left/east. This goes a little under 0.2 miles to Day Hill's summit where there's an overlook. The summit sits at 840 feet elevation, about 240 feet above the lake.

From the slab of gray stone making up the overlook, vast blue Lake Superior stretches before you. The peninsula sticking into the lake to the southwest is Corundrum Point; to the northeast is Ellingson Island and Little Two Harbors with the lighthouse looming above the bay. On a clear day, Wisconsin's Apostle Islands can be seen to the southeast.

You'll also see the remnants of an old stone fireplace. Its origins remain a mystery, but legend says that around 1900, Duluth businessman Frank Day began building a house atop the rock for he and the woman of his dreams, but when she did not return his love, he gave up on the project.

Long Loop

The short route is only a segment of the Day Hill Trail. If

you have more energy, rather than turning to head around the hill's north side, instead continue straight/southwest and swing around Day Hill's lake side.

After passing a spur trail to a cart-in campground on the lake, head right/north at the next junction. You'll then travel along the hill's southwest side below its summit.

At the next junction, which is the Gitchi-Gami State Trail, head right/northeast. Then take the next right/east trail to Day Hill's summit.

Upon coming down from the summit, go right/northeast to wrap around the base of the hill's north side. At the next junction, go left/east on the stem, heading back to the parking lot.

Little Two Harbors Trail

Great views of a famous lighthouse and of Lake Superior from a pebble beach await on the Little Two Harbors Trail.

The 3.2-mile round trip trail ranks among the most popular at the state park. To reach the trailhead, use the entry road and parking lots for the light station visitor center. Rather than go to the center, though, follow the trail heading southwest from the lot.

Initially, the trail offers access to a few of the light station's historic sites. The first junction is for a path that loops back to light station while the second junction is with a trail heading to the lake. At both intersections, continue straight/west.

In short order, the trail curves southwest. It heads downhill over a wide trail with round cobbles on it; it is a terrace formed some 9000-10,000 years ago when Glacial Lake Duluth covered this area and was some 30-40 feet higher than Lake Superior is now.

When a footbridge crosses an intermittent creek, pause to look over the sides at the angular, step-like rocks of the rock

Little Two Harbors Trail

outcrop. This is a distinctive type of basalt lava flow called Tortured Basalt because of the way the rock breaks off, which is due to weathering along the fractures crisscrossing it. The rock is best seen in late summer and autumn when water levels are low.

Asters bloom along the trail here during the same season. Most are white and purple. Bush honeysuckle and an impressive grove of birch trees also are present, as well as spruce trees.

As the trail arrives at the lake, it reaches Pebble Beach on Little Two Harbors. The protected cove is the perfect spot to take a safe swim in Lake Superior or to enjoy lunch; picnic tables are beyond the treeline along the beach. Three trail junctions across along the beach lead to the picnic area and a parking lot.

Be sure to take a gander north along the shoreline, and you'll be treated to a great view of the Split Rock Lighthouse

The century-old structure sits atop Stony Point.

At the beach's southwest end is the trail's namesake, Little Two Harbors, where a small fishing village existed about a century ago. Ellingson Island sits just offshore, and the lighthouse still is visible.

After passing a portage route to the lake – the cove is popular with kayakers – the trail curves south. There's a carry-in campsite in this area as well.

The junction with Day Hill Trail marks the end of the Little Two Harbors Trail. This is a good spot to turn back.

Split Rock Light Station Trail

Day hikers can explore one of the nation's most famous lighthouses and enjoy impressive cliff top views of Lake Superior on the Split Rock Light Station Trail.

The 0.8-mile walk is a collection of walking paths around the historic Split Rock lighthouse. Perched atop a 130-foot high solid rock cliff overlooking Lake Superior, Split Rock is among the most photographed lighthouses in the country. The Minnesota Historical Society operates the 25-acre site in Split Rock Lighthouse State Park.

To reach the lighthouse from Hwy. 61, take the main park road to parking area for Split Rock Light Station and History Center. Begin the hike at the parking lot's southeast end by taking the walking path to the visitor center. After enjoying the exhibits, head back to the parking lot's southwest end and go west on the Little Two Harbors Trail.

At the second junction, head south, taking the trail downhill to the pump house and the old dock location on the lake. When the lighthouse was being constructed and for almost a quarter century after opening, it could only be reached by water.

Initially, this required that supplies be hoisted via crane from ships to the clifftop. By 1916, though, a tramway was constructed so that supplies could be brought up in a cart with a gasoline engine powering the cables. Today, only the tramway's concrete support piers stand.

Retrace your steps to Little Two Harbors Trail and head right/east. Take the next trail heading right/south. This passes two buildings of a private residence then the restored keeper's home on the left/north.

Summer visitors can go inside the two-story brick house. It and two other grounds buildings are open from mid-May to mid-October, usually 10 a.m. to 6 p.m. The cozy first floor consists of a kitchen, dining room and living room while the upstairs has three bedrooms and a bath. A cistern is in the cellar.

Leaving the keeper's house, continue on the trail. Go right/south at the next junction to the brick fog-signal building and the lighthouse.

Visitors also can go inside the fog-signal building. When the light station opened more than a century ago, two six-inch sirens, powered by a 22-horsepower gasoline engine, warned off ships that might not be able to see the lighthouse beacon due to fog.

Next to the fog-signal building is the lighthouse, which recently was restored to its pre-1924 appearance. Summer visitors can enter the octagonal brick tower, which was built around a steel framework. The lighthouse stands 54-feet high, with a lens manufactured in France that flashed every 10 seconds. Officially, the light could be seen up to 22 miles away, but fishermen in Grand Marais more than 60 miles away, reported they could spot it on clear nights.

Take the walking trail north from the lighthouse and past the keeper's home, as if heading to the visitor center. At the next trail junction, go right/southeast past the oil house.

As the trail reaches the cliff overlooking Lake Superior, the route curves north past the old hoist location. The hoist was

Split Rock Lighthouse

used to supply the lighthouse until the tram opened, which in turn was displaced by the nearby highway.

That road wasn't constructed until 1929, and even then a driveway to the lighthouse wasn't built until 1944. Still, the road during the Great Depression began Split Rock's tourism tradition. During 1938, close to 100,000 people visited the lighthouse by parking off the road and hiking to the site. It probably was the most visited lighthouse in America during that decade, the Coast Guard reported at the time.

Following the hoist site, go straight/north at the next junction for a grand view of Lake Superior. The world's largest freshwater body of water, Lake Superior covers 31,700 square miles and reaches a depth of 1,332 feet.

After taking in the beautiful lake views, retrace your steps back to last trail junction. Once there, go right/west back to the parking lot.

The station officially closed in 1969 and in the decades since became a state park and a National Historic Landmark.

Visitors should note that while pets are allowed in the state park, they are not allowed in the historic area.

Nearby Trails

With Split Rock Lighthouse State Park tucked between Lake Superior and the high bluffs overlooking the Great Lake, the majority of day hiking trails follow the narrow strip that Minn. Hwy. 61 slices through. The land jutting into the lake and the Superior Hiking Trail traversing the bluffs and valleys cutting into them offer plenty of diverse hiking opportunities, from beaches and vistas to small waterfalls and placid rivers. The best way to locate the trails is to think of how they can be reached from Hwy. 61 as either heading southwest to Gooseberry Falls State Park or northeast to Tettegouche State Park.

Southwest of Split Rock

The section of Minn. Hwy. 61 southwest of Split Rock to Gooseberry Falls State Park is only a few miles long but boast some of the most visited and hiked trails in Minnesota. That's for good reason – among the sights are five waterfalls within a mile of another, a beach of utterly pink rock, and a moon-like landscape of billion-year-old stone.

Gitchi-Gami State Trail – Twin Points segments

Incredible views of Lake Superior await day hikers of the Gitchi-Gami State Trail between Split Rock Lighthouse and Gooseberry Falls state parks.

A 14.1-mile one–way segment of the trail heads northeast between Gooseberry Falls State Park and Beaver Bay. A good way to explore the lower half of that segment is by starting at the Twin Points Wayside.

To reach it, from Split Rock drive south on Minn. Hwy. 61. At mile marker 43, turn left/southwest into one of the two parking lots, which offers ample space.

South to Gooseberry Falls State Park

Heading southwest on the trail should start with a quick walk to the boat launch at the southwest parking lot's end. From the launch, you can access Twin Points Public Access Beach. The lot and beach used to be the sight of a Lake Superior resort.

The Gitchi-Gami can be picked up at the driveway entering the lots. Go left/southwest on the trail, which for 0.57 miles or so hugs the highway.

Next the trail swerves southeast to a quieter, wooded area away from the highway. When the trail curves southwest again, watch for and take one of the dirt paths heading

Gitchi-Gami State Trail at Twin Points

southeast; these lead to Thompson Beach, which stretches a little under a quarter mile along Lake Superior.

About 0.5 miles after leaving Hwy. 61, the Gitchi-Gami rejoins it. That spot marks a good turnback point to head back. Alternately, you can continue walking to Gooseberry Falls State Park, whose parking lot is 1.18 miles ahead with Upper

Falls along the way.

North to West Split Rock River

Alternately, from Twin Points, the trail can be hiked north to Split Rock Lighthouse State Park's West Split Rock River. It's a little more than 4-miles round trip.

From the northern parking lot, head right/northeast onto the wooded trail. The route immediately passes a connector trail to Iona's Beach, whose pink rock shoreline warrants a trip all on its own.

In a quarter mile from the parking lot, the trail again runs alongside Hwy. 61. About 0.3 miles later, it comes right up to Lake Superior. This narrow spot marks a good spot to turn back.

Alternately, you can continue walking northeast to Split Rock Lighthouse State Park. The Split Rock River DOT Wayside is in about 0.9 miles.

Iona's Beach Trail
Iona's Beach Scientific and Natural Area

Day hikers can stroll a beach of pink rock on the North Shore via the Iona's Beach Trail.

The stem trail and lakeshore at Iona's Beach Scientific and Natural Area run 0.7-miles round trip. You probably won't need to walk that far, though – the beach is a mere fifth of a mile from the parking lot.

To reach Iona's Beach, from Split Rock Lighthouse State Park drive south on Minn. Hwy. 61. At milepost 41, turn left/east into the Twin Points Public Access Beach. Veer to the parking lot on the left/north for Iona's Beach.

From the wayside lot, a rustic trail heads past towering, fragrant pines with the dappled light of the sun sifting through the branches. Part of the path to the beach is shared with the Gitchi-Gami State Trail, so be careful of not continu-

Iona's Beach

ing north on the bike trail when it splits from the route leading to the shoreline.

As closing on the beach, glimpses of Lake Superior appear
through the pines.

In a mere thousand feet from the lot, the trail opens up to
a scene out of a fairy tale – a beach of utterly pink rock, layer-
ed in wavy patterns as the baby blue waters of Lake Superior
lap against it.

Stepping onto the beach, which stretches three football
fields long, the piles of thin flat rocks crackle and crunch beneath your feet. The pink rocks come from a cliff of pink
rhyolite at the beach's north end. A point of ancient basalt at
the beach's south end prevents the pebbles – known by ge-
ologists as shingles – from drifting southward, allowing them
to pile up here.

The pinkness can be somewhat blinding. But not every
rock is that color – there are a few rare gray ones in the mix

that lovers who've previously walked here have gathered and placed into the shapes of hearts that stand out against the light rose stones.

There's also a long tree log that's been bleached to the color of chalk, and sometimes a white seagull will flit past, making its *screeeee!* call.

But mostly the beach is quiet as you sit upon the log and take in the vast lake, letting all of your worries fade with horizon.

After enjoying the sights, retrace your steps back to the parking lot.

Superior Hiking Trail, Blueberry Hill Road to Split Rock River Valley segment

Dazzling vistas of Lake Superior and massive tufts of Arctic lichen await day hikers on a segment of the Superior Hiking Trail south of Split Rock Lighthouse State Park.

After leaving Split Rock, the Superior Hiking Trail meanders for six miles across a ridge overlooking Lake Superior on its way to Gooseberry Falls State Park. This route could be treated as a point-to-point trail; another approach that is more convenient to day hikers is to split it into two sections by starting at Blueberry Hill Road.

To reach this access point, from Split Rock Lighthouse State Park, drive south on Minn. Hwy. 61. Turn right/northwest onto Blueberry Hill Road, whose dirt surface as it climbs into the forested hills quickly will have you feeling like you've truly entered a remote wilderness.

Watch closely for a break in the woods where the Superior Hiking Trail crosses the road. Park off the side of the road.

Going west toward Gooseberry Falls is peaceful but not particularly spectacular as the trail runs through birch groves at the ridge's base. Heading east, however, offers several great vistas. The somewhat challenging path starts with a steep but short climb to the top of Bread Loaf Ridge. Spectacular views of Lake Superior and the forest below abound for about a mile.

There's also a lot of rare sites to see in the forest itself.

You'll likely notice a lot of reindeer moss, a lichen that usually is found in the polar regions. On the ridge, they form hemispherical tufts about the size of a bushel basket; when that large, the moss probably is about a century old.

There's also a lot of weathered rock. These outcroppings mark the top of a series of lava flows that 1.1 billion years ago covered this section of the continent. Exposure to wind, rain, freezing and glaciers over the eons have exposed this ancient, underlying basalt at several spots on the forest floor.

You also won't be able to help but smell the wild roses when they bloom in June through July. The sweet-scented five-petaled pink flower with its yellow center stands starkly against kelly green leaves.

At 1.6 miles from trailhead, the Superior Hiking Trail descends into the Split Rock River Valley. This marks a good spot to turn back for a 3.2-mile round trip.

Should you continue on, the trail climbs back up the other side of the valley then an easy descent through a birch grove before reaching a waterfall on a branch of the Split Rock River. The waterfall is 2.7 miles (one-way) from Blueberry Hill Road but can be more easily reached by taking the Superior Hiking Trail from the Split Rock River DOT Wayside.

River View Trail

Three waterfalls and an agate beach await day hikers on Gooseberry Falls State Park's River View Trail.

The route, as described here, runs about 1.8 miles total through the heart of what many consider to be among the

most beautiful parks on the North Shore, if not all of Minnesota.

Upon entering the state park, leave your vehicle in the
first lot. Take the connector trail northeast to a walkway, on
which you'll go left/north.

A mixed evergreen, aspen, birch forest covers the park. As
hiking, don't be surprised to find enormous stumps – they're
the remains of white pines that once covered the North Shore
until logged off in the 1890s.

Upper, Middle, Lower Falls

At the next junction, go right/northeast. When the path
splits, continue right. This leads to Gooseberry River and the
Lower Falls.

A 30-foot drop, Lower Falls is the last of the waterfalls before the river flows into Lake Superior. The Gooseberry rushes over volcanic rock formed 1.1 billion years ago when lava
flows covered this part of the earth; today, they are the black
rock visible at each of the falls. When glaciers retreated about
10,000 years ago at the end of the last ice age, erosion exposed the hardened volcanic bedrock, creating the waterfalls.

The view of Lower Falls technically places you on the River View Trail. Walk left/northwest; within a few feet, you'll
come to Middle Falls, another 30-foot drop.

Continue northeast under the highway bridge, staying on
the trail that hugs the shoreline. You'll quickly arrive at Upper Falls, the third 30-foot drop on the river.

Common loons and ravens often can be spotted circling
the pools beneath the falls while herring gulls nest in col-
onies along the lakeshore. Each spring and fall, migratory
birds using the North Shore flyway arrive here in great num-
bers.

Backtrack to the highway, this time crossing the river via
the catwalk under the bridge to the other side. Continue

Middle Falls at Gooseberry Falls State Park

heading southeast, again passing Middle Falls. This side of the Gooseberry affords a better view of Lower Falls.

Agate Beach

At the next junction, continue straight, crossing the footbridge onto an island in the river's middle. Stay on the trail hugging the island's shoreline then cross the next bridge to the river's south shore.

Go left/southeast, following the trail along the river to its mouth with Lake Superior. You'll soon reach Agate Beach, where you can hunt for agates on the rocky shoreline and explore tide pools in which tadpoles often can be found.

Sometimes various species of Lake Superior salmon can be spotted in the river. Black bears, gray wolves, and white-tail deer also call the park home.

Follow the river upstream. About a half-mile from beach, take the connecting trail left/southeast and at the next trail junction go right/southwest for the parking lots.

Picnic Flow Trail

Day hikers can walk an expansive cliff of billion-year-old lava rock overlooking Lake Superior via the Picnic Flow Trail at Gooseberry Falls State Park.

The 3-mile round-trip heads to an impressive part of the state park that most visitors miss. The Picnic Flow is worth the hike, however. It'll give you the feeling of being on the moon – or if a good wind is blowing off the lake, of being on newly formed volcanic rock in Hawaii.

Use the same parking lot as for the River View Trail near the visitor's center. Leave from the lot's northeast corner, heading into a birch and spruce woods where the trail veers south, quickly crossing Camp Road near the camp registration pullout.

Once on the road's other side, continue south into a grassy area of asters, buttercups, daisies, hawkweed and Metensia. The varied colors of these wildflowers – white, yellow, orange and blue – can make for a nice show amid the green grass.

At the grassy area's south end, take the paved Gitchi-Gami State Trail right/east through the woods and to a parking lot for the Bird Ridge Group site where campers unload their vehicles. A path leads from the lot's southeast side to just north of where Pebble Creek flows into Lake Superior. Go right/southeast at the trail intersection.

In about 400 feet, the path opens onto the Picnic Lava Flow. About 1.1 billion years ago, red hot lava spread across this area in smooth and ropy swaths called a Pahoehoe flow. Such flows are common in Hawaii today. Follow this ancient basalt northeast along the lakeshore; sometimes the trail winds into the woods, especially at small bays.

Looking down at your feet, keep an eye out for amygdules, which usually are banded blues and creams and reddish-

Picnic Flow Trail

whites. These round rocks were weathered out of the basalt and can be up to a quarter in size. The white crystals in the rock are feldspar that can be up to 2 inches wide. Remember to look up, though – a steep cliff overlooks Lake Superior to the east.

Water puddles here may look like tidal pools found on Pacific Northwest coasts, but they're not formed the same way. Instead, splash water gets trapped here during storms and remains until evaporating.

Despite a moon-like barrenness, the Picnic Lava Flow is home to many plants including harebells and cinquefoil.

Once the lava flow ends, the trail heads through a grassy area and grove of mountain ash. It then comes to Agate Beach II, where orange lichen covers the bedrock. Tansies, wild roses and raspberry bushes also flourish here.

Take the stairs to the rock picnic shelter. On the shelter's right is a sea stack in the making. Common in the Pacific

Northwest, wave action creates sea stacks by separating chunks of rock from the mainland.

The overlook with the picnic shelter sits amid red pine. It offers a good view of the lake with its waves striking black basalt. When windy, the waves turn a frothy white.

A spit to the shelter's north comes and goes seasonally as the lake's breaking waves carry sand and pebbles beyond the bar while the Gooseberry River's currents bring their own sediment downstream. The two mix, forming the bar in summer through autumn with the river's heavier flow in spring washing it away.

After taking in the sights from the shelter, turn back here and retrace your steps to the parking lot.

Read about other Gooseberry Falls State Park trails in **Day Hiking Trails of Gooseberry Falls State Park**.

Northeast of Split Rock

The section of Minn. Hwy. 61 northeast of Split Rock Lighthouse to Tettegouche State Park stretches a few more miles than that heading south to Gooseberry Falls and is just as spectacular. The sights include the highest waterfall entirely in Minnesota, a cliff dramatically rising 300 feet above Lake Superior, and great vistas from the hills overlooking the lake.

Superior Hiking Trail, Beaver Bay to Cove Point segment

Another great way to experience the lengthy Superior Hiking Trail is via short segments from Beaver Bay to either eastern or western Cove Point.

The entire hike runs 6-miles round trip, though it can be shortened to half of that by stopping at a great vista of Lake Superior.

To reach the trailhead, from Split Rock Lighthouse State Park, travel north on Minn. Hwy. 61. Upon reaching the north side of Beaver Bay – the North Shore's oldest Euro-American settlement – turn left/northwest onto County Road 4/Lax Lake Road. A parking is in 0.8 miles on the road's right/north side.

After parking, carefully cross the road and head straight into the woods on the narrow Superior Hiking Trail. You'll begin with a steady climb up a slab of moss-covered bedrock. When you begin to descend this hill, you're on the backside of the ancient volcanic slab. This up and down walk over a solid rock surface repeats itself four more times between Beaver Bay and Split Rock.

The trail sports a variety of trees, including balsam, birch and maple. Cedar groves dominate in lower areas.

At 1.3 miles is a spur trail to first of two vistas – eastern

Cove Point. If looking for a short walk, head through the
birch forest to this view of Lake Superior. It's in 0.2 miles.
Turning back for the parking lot at the vista equals a 3-mile
roundtrip hike.

Alternately, you can skip that spur trail and continue
straight on the main trail to western Cove Point, which is 3
miles from the parking lot. The trail runs atop a cliff overlooking the Beaver River to the north and offers some views
of the railroad linking Iron Range taconite mines to a processing plant up the lake in Silver Bay.

The trail then turns south on the last leg to western Cove
Point, running atop Fault Line Ridge. Red pines dominate the
ridge and cliff overlooking the river. Turning back at western
Cove Point is 6-miles round trip.

Another way to reach the points is via the Cove Point Spur
Trail Loop. Start by parking at the Cove Point Lodge, cross
Hwy. 61 and head uphill. You'll head over a stream then pass
a former mink farm and a communications tower. At 1.2
miles is the first junction. Going right/north leads you to a
eastern Cove Point. Going left/west brings up to the main Superior Hiking Trail in 1.1 miles; go right/north on for 0.7
miles to western Cove Point. While part of the loop is wide,
it's an ascent the whole the way to the ridgelines where the
two points sit.

Superior Hiking Trail, Beaver River segment

The second longest segment of the Superior Hiking Trail
stretches between Split Rock Lighthouse State Park and
Beaver Bay with 10.6 miles of uninterrupted trail. While
that's a little long for a day hike, you can get a good taste of
what awaits there via a short 2-miles round trip section
along the Beaver River.

To reach the trailhead, from Split Rock Lighthouse State
Park, drive north on Minn. Hwy. 61 to Beaver Bay. One there,

turn left/north on County Road 4/Lax Lake Road. A parking lot is on the road's right/northeast side in 0.8 miles.

From the lot, head northeast on the trail. ATVs share the route for about 0.4 miles.

At that point, the trail crosses a metal bridge over the Beaver River then turns onto a footpath hugging the waterway. The Beaver River rises out of the highlands and runs 23.4 miles before spilling into Lake Superior.

Initially along the trail, the Beaver River is wide and gentle, as it flows past fragrant cedar and white pine groves. Soon, though, the river turns into a raging cascade.

The trail then comes upon two small campsites. The North Beaver River Campsite is first, and a quarter mile later is the South Beaver River Campsite.

After the south campsite a mile into the hike, the trail turns away from the Beaver River and gains elevation through a forest of birch, cedar and spruce. Given the loss of the river view and the ascent, turn back at the south campsite.

Beaver River Falls

The Superior Hiking Trail unfortunately won't get you to thundering Beaver River Falls. To see that, you'll need to head south from the parking lot on County Road 4. Just before the Hwy. 61 intersection, turn left/northeast into the falls' large parking lot.

From the lot, hike about 0.05 miles downhill to the falls. There, the river spills over ancient black rock that is around 1.09 billion years old. Several drops make up the falls, totaling about 55 feet in height.

Superior Hiking Trail, Twin Lakes segment

Day hikers can visit twin lakes nestled in the North Shore highlands on the Superior Hiking Trail.

The 7-miles round trip section of the trail passes both scenic Bean and Bear lakes, which sit northwest of Silver Bay. As the lakes are right next to one another and close in size, they often are referred to as the "Twin Lakes."

To reach the trailhead, from Split Rock Lighthouse State Park, drive north on Minn. Hwy. 61. In Silver Bay, turn left/ north onto County Road 5/Outer Drive. The road eventually becomes County Road 11/Penn Boulevard. Drive into the highlands. Turn into the parking lot on the right/north. The trailhead is in the lot's southeast corner.

Initially, an ATV trail and the Superior Hiking Trail share the same route. They split in a hundred yards with the SHT going left/north. The trail heads uphill, crossing another ATV trail then passing through a sumac stand along the way.

Next it crosses a gravel road; look to the northwest for the water tanks that supply Silver Bay. The trail then enters a spruce forest, reaches a ridgeline, and junctions with another ATV trail.

At one mile, a series of outcrops on the ridge give excellent views to the west and the south, the latter of which includes Lake Superior and Silver Bay. In 1.3 miles from the trailhead, another great vista of an oak-maple-birch tree ridge comes up.

The SHT junctions with the Twin Lakes Trail at 1.8 miles. The Twin Lakes Trail begins in Silver Bay at the Bay Area Historical Society's information center, taking the Silver Bay Spur of the Superior Hiking Trail to a loop running along the shores of Bean and Bear lakes. You're now on that loop, too. Go left/northeast and continue to the lakes.

After crossing a footbridge over Penn Creek and a spur to the Penn Creek Campsite, the trail enters pretty Superior National Forest. On the south face of the highlands, you'll find maples. Once passing outcrops, the woods turns to oak and sumac with blueberries and juneberries in the undergrowth. There's also a wetlands with a small pond to the left/west.

Next the trail heads atop high cliffs with the twin lakes to the northwest. You'll first pass about 200 feet above sparkling Bean Lake. Thirty-two acres in size and the larger of the twins, deep Bean Lake is a popular spot to catch rainbow trout.

At 2.6 miles is the Bean Lake overlook. In addition to the lake, look northeast for Mount Trudee, whose flat top covered in red pines will be visible.

Upon coming to Bear Lake, you can scramble down to its blue shores via a 150-yard (one-way) spur trail to the Bear Lake Campsite. This places you at 3.5 miles from the trailhead.

As ascending to the lakeshore, you'll be able to see Bean Lake in the distance. Any of the rocky outcrops over the lakes make for a great picnic spot.

After taking in the scenery, retrace yours steps back to the Penn Boulevard parking lot.

Note: The Twin Lakes Trail starting in Silver Bay, while scenic, runs about a half-mile longer than the route described here and involves more elevation gain, as it starts at the base of the highlands.

Gitchi-Gami State Trail, Split Rock to Silver Bay segments

While always great for bicyclists, some segments of the Gitchi-Gami State Trail are not so wonderful for hikers. The trail north from Split Rock Lighthouse State Park to Silver Bay is one such stretch.

For most of that segment, the state trail hugs Minn. Hwy. 61 or takes a couple of brief diversions alongside local roads. This makes for a noisy walk with lots of wind from fast-moving vehicles as they pass.

Still, for those who want to walk a flat, paved trail that is just as pretty as what any anyone driving Hwy. 61 would see – and it is an extremely scenic drive of pines, forested uplands, and Lake Superior views – the Gitchi-Gami is a good option.

A couple of segments in particular stand out.

In Beaver Bay, start at the north end of the 14.1-mile trail that runs through Split Rock to Gooseberry Falls State Park. Begin in downtown Beaver Bay off of Hwy. 61 south/west of Slater Drive. Hike the trail as far south as you like; the creek south of Pine Bay Loop makes a good turnback point for a little more than 4-mile round trip.

From the Silver Bay trailhead, the trail can be hiked south. Park in the trailhead lot on Penn Boulevard and head 2.3 miles (4.6-miles round trip) south/west to West Road in Beaver Bay.

The Beaver Bay and Silver Bay segments do not connect.

In addition, the Silver Bay trailhead is as far north hikers can go on the trail to Tettegouche State Park. The next segment of the Gitchi-Gami State Trail begins at the Minnesota DOT wayside in Schroeder, north of Tettegouche.

Palisade Head Trail
Tettegouche State Park

Hikers can walk atop an ancient 300-foot cliff overlooking Lake Superior at Palisade Head.

The head offers about 4000 feet of frontage above the lake. It is located within Tettegouche State Park but is not contiguous with the main park area.

To reach the trailhead, from Split Rock Lighthouse State Park, travel north on Minn. Hwy. 61 through Silver Bay. Near milepost 57, turn right/east onto a steep, narrow road that climbs to Palisade Head's top. A parking lot is close to the cliff edge next to a large radio tower.

There are no designated paths, but white spruce, aspen, mountain ash, paper birch, and oak trees grow sparsely atop the hard, erosion-resistant rock, so you can walk among them. You'll be rewarded with fantastic views of the world's largest freshwater lake. Shovel Point, which is made of the same rock as the head, can be seen about two miles distant to the northeast. Split Rock Lighthouse is to the southwest. On the clearest days, Wisconsin's Apostle Islands and the Bay-field Peninsula can be seen to the south across the lake.

The rock beneath your feet is called rhyolite. The entire palisade head is the hardened remains of a massive lava flow from about 1.1 billion years ago; at the head, the flow stretches about three miles long and two miles wide. Not only is walking across such old rock a rarity but so are rhyolite lava flows in general – only three have been recorded worldwide since 1900.

The great vista almost certainly will include a variety of raptors. Peregrine falcons nest on the head while bald eagles nest nearby. Each fall, thousands of hawks from a variety of species migrate along this shoreline.

As walking along the head, also keep an eye out for wild blueberry bushes. The berries usually come out in late July through mid-August.

Except at the parking lot, there are no railings, so watch for the edges that fall straight into the lake. This is not a great place to let young or careless children roam free.

Shovel Point Trail
Tettegouche State Park

An incredible view of Lake Superior atop billion-year-old rock awaits day hikers on the Shovel Point Trail in Tette-gouche State Park.

The North Shore hike runs about 1.1-miles round trip. A fairly flat trail, it's a wonderful autumn walk when the shoreline leaves turn an array of yellows.

To reach the trailhead from Split Rock Lighthouse State Park, drive north on Minn. Hwy. 61. After crossing the Baptism River, turn right/southeast into the park entrance. Go straight on the park entrance road and veer left into the northernmost lot. From the lot's southeastern corner, pick up the interpretive trail that heads toward Lake Superior.

The trail runs through a forested area of birch and aspen. A few pines are mixed in.

Within short order, the trail comes to the lake near a small rocky point with an overlook of the vast blue waters.

No matter what the season, you're certain to find shorebirds flying over the lake and trail. During late May as birds migrate north, up to 150 different species can be spotted.

In summer, bald eagles, peregrine falcons, and several varieties of wood warblers call the shore home.

Throughout autumn, the migration south moves at a steady pace. It usually begins in late August with flocks of the common nighthawk filling the warm evening skies. In early September, songbirds make their way through the area, and by mid-month through early October, various raptors make their push. Late October usually sees the arrival of Arctic birds.

From there, the trail veers northeast. Upon coming to the next overlook, the trail splits into a loop. Go right/southeast onto Shovel Point.

The point is the dramatic remains of 1.1-billion-year-old lava flows that were rich in rhyolite, a light-colored volcanic rock. Extremely resistant to erosion, the rock has held out through the eons against several glaciers and the lakes they've left, including cold Lake Superior, which it rises about 200 feet above.

Upon reaching the next overlook, which leaves the green forest for the beige rocks, you've come to the trail's farthest incursion on the point. You may spend a good amount of the hike simply standing in awe here as the vast lake and a shoreline of sea caves, a sea stack, the Baptism River's mouth, and Palisade Head stretch before you.

From the overlook, the trail curves around its loop through the woods back to where it split. From there, retrace your steps back to the parking lot.

If hiking with children, make sure they stay on the trail and in sight, as the cliff edges are long, straight drops.

High Falls Trail
Tettegouche State Park

A trail to a 70-foot high waterfall awaits day hikers in Tettegouche State Park.

The High Falls Trail, including a couple of spurs, runs 3.2-mile round trip, as it heads past three falls and rapids. Though unnamed on park maps, the popular trail is christened here after what most hiker taking it come to see – the High Falls.

To reach the trailhead, from Split Rock Lighthouse State Park drive north on Minn. Hwy. 61. After crossing the Baptism River, turn right/southeast into the park. Veer right/south on the park road and pass the visitor center, heading into a wooded area. Park in the pullout lot on the road's right /northwest side. You can pick up the trailhead on the lot's southwest side.

Take a right onto the trail, heading northwest. The trail goes under Hwy. 61 and parallels the Baptism River.

A short spur heads to the scenic river's shore. The Baptism runs a mere 8.8 miles, as it flows from the Minnesota Arrowhead's uplands then through a gorge of ancient rock into Lake Superior.

From the spur, the main trail curves northeast and quickly gains in elevation until it follows the rim overlooking the

High Falls

Baptism River gorge.

Below the rim are the Cascades, a set of rapids in the Baptism River. The hard black rock the river tumbles through is more than a billion years old.

Farther up the river, the trail passes Two Steps Falls, a pair of small waterfalls that flow into a large pool. The pool then drains downhill as the river rushes toward Lake Superior. A spur trial leads downhill to an overlook of the falls.

Continuing north on the main trail, the route reaches the Superior Hiking Trail. Go left/west on that trail to High Falls.

One of four waterfalls in the park, High Falls is an impressive sight as it drops more than six stories over a black basalt cliff capped by stately evergreens.

There is some controversy over the bragging rights to the highest waterfall in Minnesota. Some would argue the tallest is the 120-foot High Falls on the Pigeon River in Grand Portage State Park. As part of that waterfalls is technically in Ontario, however, the same-named High Falls on the Baptism River sometimes is advertised as "the highest waterfall entirely within Minnesota."

A trail bridge crosses the Baptism above the falls, offering a dramatic view of the river valley below. The bridge also marks a good spot to turn around on this out-and-back trail.

Best Trails Lists

Which trails are the best for watching birds? To enjoy fall colors? For its great vistas? Here are some lists of the best Split Rock Lighthouse State Park trails for those and many other specific interests (italicized trails are outside of the park).

Autumn leaves
• Split Rock Creek Trail
• *Shovel Point Trail*
• *Superior Hiking Trail, Beaver Bay to Cove Point segment*

Beaches
• Little Two Harbors Trail
• Corundum Mine Trail
• *Iona's Beach Trail*

Birdwatching
• Corundum Mine Trail
• *River View Trail*
• *Shovel Point Trail*

Campgrounds
• Day Hill Trail (cart-in)
• *High Falls Trail* (Baptism River Campground)
• *Picnic Flow Trail* (Gooseberry Falls State Park Campground)

Geology
• Corundum Mine Trail

- Split Rock River Trail
- Day Hill Trail
- *Palisade Head Trail*
- *High Falls Trail*

History/Archeology
- Corundum Mine Trail
- Merrill Logging Trail
- Split Rock Light Station Trail

Lake Superior views
- Little Two Harbors Trail
- Split Rock Light Station Trail
- *Palisade Head Trail*
- *Shovel Point Trail*

Must-do's
- Little Two Harbors Trail
- Split Rock Light Station Trail
- Split Rock River Trail
- *River View Trail*
- *Shovel Point Trail*

Picnicking
- Split Rock River Trail
- Corundum Mine Trail
- Little Two Harbors Trail
- *Picnic Flow Trail*

Plant communities
- Split Rock Creek Trail
- *Picnic Flow Trail*
- *Superior Hiking Trail, Blueberry Hill Road to Split Rock River Valley segment*

Primitive trails
• Superior Hiking Trail (any segment)

Vistas
• Day Hill Trail
• Split Rock Light Station Trail
• *Palisade Hill Trail*

Waterfalls
• Split Rock River Trail
• *High Falls Trail*
• *River View Trail*

Wildflowers
• Split Rock Creek Trail
• *Superior Hiking Trail, Blueberry Hill Road to Split Rock River Valley segment*
• *Picnic Flow Trail*

Wildlife
• Split Rock Creek Trail
• *River View Trail*
• *Shovel Point Trail*

Bonus Section:
Day Hiking Primer

Y ou'll get more out of a day hike if you research it and plan ahead. It's not enough to just pull over to the side of the road and hit a trail that you've never been on and have no idea where it goes. In fact, doing so invites disaster.

Instead, you should preselect a trail (This book's trail descriptions can help you do that). You'll also want to ensure that you have the proper clothing, equipment, navigational tools, first-aid kit, food and water. Knowing the rules of the trail and potential dangers along the way also are helpful. In this special section, we'll look at each of these topics to ensure you're fully prepared.

Selecting a Trail

For your first few hikes, stick to short, well-known trails where you're likely to encounter others. Once you get a feel for hiking, your abilities, and your interests, expand to longer and more remote trails.

Always check to see what the weather will be like on the trail you plan to hike. While an adult might be able to withstand wind and a sprinkle here or there, for kids it can be pure misery. Dry, pleasantly warm days with limited wind always are best when hiking with children.

Don't choose a trail that is any longer than the least fit person in your group can hike. Adults in good shape can go 8-12 miles a day; for kids, it's much less. There's no magical number.

When planning the hike, try to find a trail with a mid-point payoff – that is something you and definitely any children will find exciting about half-way through the hike. This will help keep up everyone's energy and enthusiasm during the journey.

If you have children in your hiking party, consider a couple of additional points when selecting a trail.

Until children enter their late teens, they need to stick to trails rather than going off-trail hiking, which is known as bushwhacking. Children too easily can get lost when off trail. They also can easily get scratched and cut up or stumble across poisonous plants and dangerous animals.

Generally, kids will prefer a circular route to one that requires hiking back the way you came. The return trip often feels anti-climatic, but you can overcome that by mentioning features that all of you might want to take a closer look at.

Once you select a trail, it's time to plan for your day hike. Doing so will save you a lot of grief – and potentially prevent an emergency – later on. You are, after all, entering the wilds, a place where help may not be readily available.

When planning your hike, follow these steps:

• Print a road map showing how to reach the parking lot near the trailhead. Outline the route with a transparent yellow highlighter and write out the directions.

• Print a satellite photo of the parking area and the trailhead. Mark the trailhead on the photo.

• Print a topo map of the trail. Outline the trail with the yellow highlighter. Note interesting features you want to see along the trail and the destination.

• If carrying GPS, program this information into your device.

• Make a timeline for your trip, listing: when you will leave home; when you will arrive at the trailhead; your turn back time; when you will return for home in your vehicle; and when you will arrive at your home.

• Estimate how much water and food you will need to bring based on the amount of time you plan to spend on the trail and in your vehicle. You'll need at least two pints of water per person for every hour on the trail.

• Fill out two copies of a hiker's safety form. Leave one in your vehicle.

• Share all of this information with a responsible person remaining in civilization, leaving a hiker's safety form with them. If they do not hear from you within an hour of when you plan to leave the trail in your vehicle, they should contact authorities to report you as possibly lost.

Clothing
Footwear

If your feet hurt, the hike is over, so getting the right footwear is worth the time. Making sure the footwear fits before hitting the trail also is worth it. With children, if you've gone a few weeks without hiking, that's plenty of time for feet to grow, and they may have just outgrown their hiking boots. Check out everyone's footwear a few days before heading out on the hike. If it doesn't fit, replace it.

For flat, smooth, dry trails, sneakers and cross-trainers are fine; but if you really want to head onto less traveled roads or tackle areas that aren't typically dry, you'll need hiking boots. Once you start doing any rocky or steep trails – and remember that a trail you consider moderately steep needs to be only half that angle for a child to consider it extremely steep – you'll want hiking boots, which offer rugged tread perfect for handling rough trails.

Socks

Socks serve two purposes: to wick sweat away from skin

and to provide cushioning. Cotton socks aren't very good for hiking, except in extremely dry environments, because they retain moisture that can lead to blisters. Wool socks or liner socks work best. You'll want to look for three-season socks, also known as trekking socks. While a little thicker than summer socks, their extra cushioning generally prevents blisters. Also, make sure kids don't put on holey socks; that's just inviting blisters.

Layering

On all but hot, dry days, when hiking you should wear multiple layers of clothing that provide various levels of protection against sweat, heat loss, wind and potentially rain. Layering works because the type of clothing you select for each stratum serves a different function, such as wicking moisture or shielding against wind. In addition, trapped air between each layer of clothing is warmed by your body heat. Layers also can be added or taken off as needed.

Generally, you need three layers. Closest to your skin is the wicking layer, which pulls perspiration away from the body and into the next layer, where it evaporates. Exertion from walking means you will sweat and generate heat, even if the weather is cold. The second layer provides insulation, which helps keep you warm. The last layer is a water-resistant shell that protects you from rain, wind, snow and sleet.

As the seasons and weather change, so does the type of clothing you select for each layer. The first layer ought to be a loose-fitting T-shirt in summer, but in winter and on other cold days you might opt for a long-sleeved moisture-wicking synthetic material, like polypropylene. During winter, the next layer probably also should cover the neck, which often is exposed to the elements. A turtleneck works fine, but preferably not one made of cotton. The third layer in winter, depending on the temperature, could be a wool sweater, a half-zippered long sleeved fleece jacket, or a fleece vest.

You might even add a fourth layer of a hooded parka with pockets, made of material that can block wind and resist water. Gloves or mittens as well as a hat also are necessary on cold days.

Headgear

Half of all body heat is lost through the head, hence the hiker's adage, "If your hands are cold, wear a hat." In cool, wet weather, wearing a hat is at least good for avoiding hypothermia, a potentially deadly condition in which heat loss occurs faster than the body can generate it. Children are more susceptible to hypothermia than adults.

Especially during summer, a hat with a wide brim is useful in keeping the sun out of eyes. It's also nice should rain start falling.

For young children, get a hat with a chin strap. They like to play with their hats, which will fly off in a wind gust if not fastened some way to the child.

Sunglasses

Sunglasses are an absolute must if walking through open areas exposed to the sun and in winter when you can suffer from snow blindness. Look for 100% UV-protective shades, which provide the best screen.

Equipment

A couple of principles should guide your purchases. First, the longer and more complex the hike, the more equipment you'll need. Secondly, your general goal is to go light. Since you're on a day hike, the amount of gear you'll need is a fraction of what backpackers shown in magazines and catalogues usually carry. Still, the inclination of most day hikers is to not carry enough equipment. For the lightness is-sue, most gear today is made with titanium and siliconized nylon, ensuring it is sturdy yet fairly light. While the following list of what you need may look long, it won't weigh much.

Backpacks

Sometimes called daypacks (for day hikes or for kids), backpacks are essential to carry all of the essentials you need – snacks, first-aid kit, extra clothing.

For day hiking, you'll want to get yourself an internal frame, in which the frame giving the backpack its shape is in-side the pack's fabric so it's not exposed to nature. Such frames usually are lightweight and comfortable.

External frames have the frame outside the pack, so they are exposed to the elements. They are excellent for long hikes into the backcountry when you must carry heavy loads, however.

As kids get older, and especially after they've been hiking for a couple of years, they'll want a "real" backpack. Unfor-tunately, most backpacks for kids are overbuilt and too heavy. Even light ones that safely can hold up to 50 pounds are inane for most children.

When buying a daypack for your child, look for sternum straps, which help keep the strap on the shoulders. This is vital for prepubescent children, as they do not have the broad shoulders that come with adolescence, meaning packs likely will slip off and onto their arms, making them uncom-fortable and difficult to carry. Don't buy a backpack that a child will "grow into." Backpacks that don't fit well simply will lead to sore shoulder and back muscles and could result in poor posture.

Also, consider purchasing a daypack with a hydration system for kids. This will help ensure they drink a lot of water. More on this later when we get to canteens.

Before hitting the trail, always check your children's backpacks to make sure that they have not overloaded them. Kids think they need more than they really do. They also tend to overestimate their own ability to carry stuff. Sibling rivalries often lead to children packing more than they should in their rucksacks, too. Don't let them overpack "to teach them a lesson," though, as it can damage bones and turn the hike into a bad experience.

A good rule of thumb is no more than 25 percent capacity. Most upper elementary school kids can carry only about 10 pounds for any short distance. Subtract the weight of the backpack, and that means only 4-5 pounds in the backpack. Overweight children will need to carry a little less than this or they'll quickly be out of breath.

Child carriers

If your child is an infant or toddler, you'll have to carry him. Until infants can hold their heads up, which usually doesn't happen until about four to six months of age, a front pack (like a Snugli or Baby Bjorn) is best. It keeps the infant close for warmth and balances out your backpack. At the same time, though, you must watch for baby overheating in a front pack, so you'll need to remove the infant from your body at rest stops.

Once children reach about 20 pounds, they typically can hold their heads up and sit on their own. At that point, you'll want a baby carrier (sometimes called a child carrier or baby backpack), which can transfer the infant's weight to your hips when you walk. You'll not only be comfortable, but your child will love it, too.

Look for a baby carrier that is sturdy yet lightweight. Your child is going to get heavier as time passes, so about the only way you can counteract this is to reduce the weight of the items you use to carry things. The carrier also should have adjustment points, as you don't want your child to outgrow the carrier too soon. A padded waist belt and padded shoulder straps are necessary for your comfort. The carrier should provide some kind of head and neck support if you're hauling an infant. It also should offer back support for children of all ages, and leg holes should be wide enough so there's no chafing. You want to be able to load your infant without help, so it should be stable enough to stand that way when you take it off the child can sit in it for a moment while you get turned around. Stay away from baby carriers with only shoulder straps as you need the waist belt to help shift the child's weight to your hips for more comfortable walking.

Fanny packs

Also known as a belt bag, a fanny pack is virtually a must for anyone with a baby carrier as you can't otherwise lug a backpack. If your significant other is with you, he or she can carry the backpack, of course. Still, the fanny pack also is a good alternative to a backpack in hot weather, as it will reduce back sweat. If you have only one or two kids on a hike, or if they also are old enough to carry daypacks, your fanny pack need not be large. A mid-size pouch can carry at least 200 cubic inches of supplies, which is more than enough to accommodate all the materials you need. A good fanny pack also has a spot for hooking canteens to.

Canteens

Canteens or plastic bottles filled with water are vital for any hike, no matter how short the trail. You'll need to have enough of them to carry about two pints of water per person for every hour of hiking.

Trekking poles

Also known as walking poles or walking sticks, trekking

poles are necessary for maintaining stability on uneven or wet surfaces and to help reduce fatigue. The latter makes them useful on even surfaces. By transferring weight to the arms, a trekking pole can reduce stress on knees and lower back, allowing you to maintain a better posture and to go farther.

If an adult with a baby or toddler on your back, you'll primarily want a trekking pole to help you maintain your balance, even if on a flat surface, and to help absorb some of the impact of your step.

Graphite tips provide the best traction. A basket just above the tip is a good idea so the stick doesn't sink into mud or sand. Angled cork handles are ergonomic and help absorb sweat from your hands so they don't blister. A strap on the handle to wrap around your hand is useful so the stick doesn't slip out. Telescopic poles are a good idea as you can adjust them as needed based on the terrain you're hiking and as kids grow to accommodate their height.

The pole also needs to be sturdy enough to handle rugged terrain, as you don't want a pole that bends when you press it to the ground. Spring-loaded shock absorbers help when heading down a steep incline but aren't necessary. Indeed, for a short walk across flat terrain, the right length stick is about all you need.

Carabiners

Carabiners are metal loops, vaguely shaped like a D, with a sprung or screwed gate. You'll find that hooking a couple of them to your backpack or fanny pack useful in many ways. For example, if you need to dig through a fanny pack, you can hook the strap of your trekking pole to it. Your hat, camera straps, first-aid kit, and a number of other objects also can connect to them. Hook carabiners to your fanny pack or backpack upon purchasing them so you don't forget them when packing. Small carabiners with sprung gates are inexpensive, but they do have a limited life span of a couple of dozen hikes.

Navigational Tools

Paper maps

Paper maps may sound passé in this age of GPS, but you'll find the variety and breadth of view they offer to be useful. During the planning process, a paper map (even if viewing it online), will be far superior to a GPS device. On the hike, you'll also want a backup to GPS. Or like many casual hikers, you may not own GPS at all, which makes paper maps indispensable.

Standard road maps (which includes printed guides and handmade trail maps) show highways and locations of cities and parks. Maps included in guidebooks, printed guides handed out at parks, and those that are hand-drawn tend to be designed like road maps, and often carry the same positives and negatives.

Topographical maps give contour lines and other important details for crossing a landscape. You'll find them invaluable on a hike into the wilds. The contour lines' shape and their spacing on a topo map show the form and steepness of a hill or bluff, unlike the standard road map and most brochures and hand-drawn trail maps. You'll also know if you're in a woods, which is marked in green, or in a clearing, which is marked in white. If you get lost, figuring out where you are and how to get to where you need to be will be much easier with such information.

Satellite photos offer a view from above that is rendered exactly as it would look from an airplane. Thanks to Google and other online services, you can get fairly detailed pictures of the landscape. Such pictures are an excellent resource when researching a hiking trail. Unfortunately, those pictures don't label what a feature is or what it's called, as would a topo map. Unless there's a stream, determining if a feature is a valley bottom or a ridgeline also can be difficult. Like topo maps, satellite photos (most of which were taken by old Russian spy satellites), can be out of date a few years.

GPS

By using satellites, the global positioning system can find your spot on the Earth to within 10 feet. With a GPS device, you can preprogram the trailhead location and mark key turns and landmarks as well as the hike's end point. This mobile map is a powerful technological tool that almost certainly ensures you won't get lost – so long as you've correctly programmed the information. GPS also can calculate travel time and act as a compass, a barometer and altimeter, making such devices virtually obsolete on a hike.

In remote areas, however, reception is spotty at best for GPS, rendering your mobile map worthless. A GPS device also runs on batteries, and there's always a chance they will go dead. Or you may drop your device, breaking it in the process. Their screens are small, and sometimes you need a large paper map to get a good sense of the natural landmarks around you.

Compass

Like a paper map, a compass is indispensable even if you use GPS. Should your GPS no longer function, the compass then can be used to tell you which direction you're heading. A protractor compass is best for hiking. Beneath the compass needle is a transparent base with lines to help your orient yourself.

The compass often serves as a magnifying glass to help you make out map details. Most protractor compasses also come with a lanyard for easy carrying.

Food and Water

Water

As water is the heaviest item you'll probably carry, there is a temptation to not take as much as one should. Don't skimp on the amount of water you bring, though; after all, it's the one supply your body most needs. It's always better to end up having more water than you needed than returning to your vehicle dehydrated.

How much water should you take? Adults need at least a quart for every two hours hiking. Children need to drink about a quart every two hours of walking and more if the weather is hot or dry. To keep kids hydrated, have them drink at every rest stop.

Don't presume there will be water on the hiking trail. Most trails outside of urban areas lack such amenities. In addition, don't drink water from local streams, lakes, rivers or ponds. There's no way to tell if local water is safe or not. As soon as you have consumed half of your water supply, you should turn around for the vehicle.

Food

Among the many wonderful things about hiking is that snacking between meals isn't frowned upon. Unless going on an all-day hike in which you'll picnic along the way, you want to keep everyone in your hiking party fed, especially as hunger can lead to lethargic and discontented children. It'll also keep young kids from snacking on the local flora or dirt. Before hitting the trail, you'll want to repackage as much of the food as possible as products sold at grocery stores tend to come in bulky packages that take up space and add a little weight to your backpack. Place the food in re-sealable plastic bags.

Bring a variety of small snacks for rest stops. You don't want kids filling up on snacks, but you do need them to maintain their energy levels if they're walking or to ensure they don't turn fussy if riding in a child carrier. Go for complex carbohydrates and proteins for maintaining energy. Good options include dried fruits, jerky, nuts, peanut butter, prepared energy bars, candy bars with a high protein content (nuts, peanut butter), crackers, raisins and trail mix (called "gorp"). A number of trail mix recipes are available online; you and your children may want to try them out at home to see which ones you collectively like most.

Salty treats rehydrate better than sweet treats do. Chocolate and other sweets are fine if they're not all that's exclusively served, but remember they also tend to lead to thirst and to make sticky messes. Whichever snacks you choose, don't experiment with food on the trail. Bring what you know kids will like.

Give the first snack within a half-hour of leaving the trailhead or you risk children becoming tired and whiny from low energy levels. If kids start asking for them every few steps even after having something to eat at the last rest stop, consider timing snacks to reaching a seeable landmark, such as, "We'll get out the trail mix when we reach that bend up ahead."

Milk for infants

If you have an infant or unweaned toddler with you, milk is as necessary as water. Children who only drink breastfed milk but don't have their mother on the hike require that you have breast-pumped milk in an insulated beverage container (such as a Thermos) that can keep it cool to avoid spoiling. Know how much the child drinks and at what frequency so you can bring enough. You'll also need to carry the child's bottle and feeding nipples. Bring enough extra water in your canteen so you can wash out the bottle after each feeding. A handkerchief can be used to dry bottles between feedings.

Don't forget the baby's pacifier. Make sure it has a string and hook attached so it connects to the baby's outfit and isn't lost.

What not to bring

Avoid soda and other caffeinated beverages, alcohol, and energy pills. The caffeine will dehydrate children as well as you. Alcohol has no place on the trail; you need your full faculties when making decisions and driving home. Energy pills essentially are a stimulant and like alcohol can lead to bad calls. If you're tired, get some sleep and hit the trail another day.

First-aid Kit

After water, this is the most essential item you can carry.

A first-aid kit should include:

• Adhesive bandages of various types and sizes, especially butterfly bandages (for younger kids, make sure they're colorful kid bandages)

• Aloe vera

• Anesthetic (such as Benzocaine)

• Antacid (tablets)

• Antibacterial (aka antibiotic) ointment (such as Neosporin or Bacitracin)

• Anti-diarrheal tablets (for adults only, as giving this to a child is controversial)

• Anti-itch cream or calamine lotion

• Antiseptics (such as hydrogen peroxide, iodine or Betadine, Mercuroclear, rubbing alcohol)

• Baking soda

• Breakable (or instant) ice packs

• Cotton swabs

• Disposable syringe (w/o needle)

• Epipen (if children or adults have allergies)

• Fingernail clippers (your multi-purpose tool might have this, and if so you can dispense with it)
   • Gauze bandage
   • Gauze compress pads (2x2 individually wrapped pad)
   • Hand sanitizer (use this in place of soap)
   • Liquid antihistamine (not Benadryl tablets, however, as children should take liquid not pills; be aware that liquid antihistamines may cause drowsiness)
   • Medical tape
   • Moisturizer containing an anti-inflammatory
   • Mole skin
   • Pain reliever (aka aspirin; for children's pain relief, use liquid acetaminophen such Tylenol or liquid ibuprofen; never give aspirin to a child under 12)
   • Poison ivy cream (for treatment)
   • Poison ivy soap
   • Powdered sports drinks mix or electrolyte additives
   • Sling
   • Snakebite kit
   • Thermometer
   • Tweezers (your multi-purpose tool may have this allowing you to dispense with it)
   • Water purification tablets

If infants are with you, be sure to also carry teething ointment (such as Orajel) and diaper rash treatment.

Many of the items should be taken out of their store packaging to make placement in your fanny pack or backpack easier. In addition, small amounts of some items – such as baking soda and cotton swabs – can be placed inside re-sealable plastic bags, since you won't need the whole amount purchased.

Make sure the first-aid items are in a waterproof container. A re-sealable plastic zipper bag is perfectly fine. As the North Shore sports a humid climate, be sure to replace the adhesive bandages every couple of months, as they can deteriorate in the moistness. Also, check your first-aid kit every few trips and after any hike in which you've just used it, so that you can replace used components and to make sure medicines haven't expired.

If you have older elementary-age kids and teenagers who've been trained in first aid, giving them a kit to carry as well as yourself is a good idea. Should they find themselves lost or if you cannot get to them for a few moments, the kids might need to provide very basic first aid to one another.

Hiking with Children: Attitude Adjustment

To enjoy hiking with kids, you'll first have to adopt your child's perspective. Simply put, we must learn to hike on our kids' schedules – even though they may not know that's what we're doing.

Compared to adults, kids can't walk as far, they can't walk as fast, and they will grow bored more quickly. Every step we take requires three for them. In addition, early walkers, up to two years of age, prefer to wander than to "hike." Preschool kids will start to walk the trail, but at a rate of only about a mile per hour. With stops, that can turn a three-mile hike into a four-hour journey. Kids also won't be able to hike as steep of trails as you or handle as inclement of weather as you might.

This all may sound limiting, especially to long-time backpackers used to racking up miles or bagging peaks on their hikes, but it's really not. While you may have to put off some backcountry and mountain climbing trips for a while, it also opens up to you a number of great short trails and nature hikes with spectacular sights that you may have otherwise skipped because they weren't challenging enough.

So sure, you'll have to make some compromises, but the payout is high. You're not personally on the hike to get a workout but to spend quality time with your children.

Family Dog

Dogs are part of the family, and if you have children, they'll want to share the hiking experience with their pets. In turn, dogs will have a blast on the trail, some larger dogs can be used as Sherpas, and others will defend against threatening animals.

But there is a downside to dogs. Many will chase animals and so run the risk of getting lost or injured. Also, a doggy bag will have to be carried for dog pooh – yeah, it's natural, but also inconsiderate to leave for other hikers to smell and for their kids to step in. In addition, most dogs almost always will lose a battle against a threatening animal, so there's a price to be paid for your safety.

Many places where you'll hike solve the dilemma for you as dogs aren't allowed on their trails. Dogs are verboten on some Wisconsin state parks trails but usually permitted on those in national forests. Always check with the park ranger before heading to the trail.

If you can bring a dog, make sure it is well behaved and friendly to others. You don't need your dog biting another hiker while unnecessarily defending its family.

Rules of the Trail

Ah, the woods or a wide open meadow, peaceful and quiet, not a single soul around for miles. Now you and your children can do whatever you want.

Not so fast.

Act like wild animals on a hike, and you'll destroy the very aspects of the wilds that make them so attractive. You're also likely to end up back in civilization, specifically an emergency room. And there are other people around. Just as you would wish them to treat you courteously, so you and your children should do the same for them.

Let's cover how to act civilized out in the wilds.

Minimize damage to your surroundings

When on the trail, follow the maxim of "Leave no trace." Obviously, you shouldn't toss litter on the ground, start rock-slides, or pollute water supplies. How much is damage and how much is good-natured exploring is a gray area, of course. Most serious backpackers will say you should never pick up objects, break branches, throw rocks, pick flowers, and so on – the idea is not to disturb the environment at all.

Good luck getting a four-year-old to think like that. The good news is a four-year-old won't be able to throw around many rocks or break many branches.

Still, children from their first hike into the wilderness should be taught to respect nature and to not destroy their environment. While you might overlook a preschooler hurl-ing rocks into a puddle, they can be taught to sniff rather than pick flowers. As they grow older, you can teach them the value of leaving the rock alone. Regardless of age, don't allow children to write on boulders or carve into trees.

Many hikers split over picking berries. To strictly abide by the "minimize damage" principle, you wouldn't pick any ber-ries at all. Kids, however, are likely to find great pleasure in eating blackberries, currants and thimbleberries as ambling down the trail. Personally, I don't see any problem enjoying a few berries if the long-term payoff is a respect and love for nature. To minimize damage, teach them to only pick berries they can reach from the trail so they don't trample plants or deplete food supplies for animals. They also should only pick what they'll eat.

Collecting is another issue. In national and most state and county parks, taking rocks, flower blossoms and even pine cones is illegal. Picking flowers moves many species, especially if they are rare and native, one step closer to extinction. Archeological ruins are extremely fragile, and even touching them can damage a site.

But on many trails, especially gem trails, collecting is part of the adventure. Use common sense – if the point of the trail is to find materials to collect, such as a gem trail, take judiciously, meaning don't overcollect. Otherwise, leave it there.

Sometimes the trail crosses private land. If so, walking around fields, not through them, always is best or you could damage a farmer's crops.

Pack out what you pack in

Set the example as a parent: Don't litter yourself; whenever stopping, pick up whatever you've dropped; and always require kids to pick up after themselves when they litter. In the spirit of "Leave no trace," try to leave the trail cleaner than you found it, so if you come across litter that's safe to pick up, do so and bring it back to a trash bin in civilization. Given this, you may want to bring a plastic bag to carry out garbage.

Picking up litter doesn't just mean gum and candy wrappers but also some organic materials that take a long time to decompose and aren't likely to be part of the natural environment you're hiking. In particular, these include peanut shells, orange peelings, and eggshells.

Burying litter, by the way, isn't viable. Either animals or erosion soon will dig it up, leaving it scattered around the trail and woods.

Stay on the trail

Hiking off trail means potentially damaging fragile growth. Following this rule not only ensures you minimize damage but is also a matter of safety. Off trail is where kids most likely will encounter dangerous animals and poisonous plants. Not being able to see where they're stepping also increases the likelihood of falling and injuring themselves. Leaving the trail raises the chances of getting lost. Staying on the trail also means staying out of caves, mines or abandoned structures you may encounter. They are usually dangerous places.

Finally, never let children take a shortcut on a switchback trail. Besides putting them on steep ground upon which they could slip, their impatient act will cause the switchback to erode.

Trail Dangers

On Split Rock Lighthouse State Park trails, two common dangers face hikers: ticks and poison ivy/sumac. Both can make miserable your time on the trail or once back home. Fortunately, both threats are easily avoidable and treatable.

Ticks

One of the greatest dangers comes from the smallest of creatures: ticks. Both the wood and the deer tick are common in Split Rock Lighthouse State Park and can infect people with Lyme disease.

Ticks usually leap onto people from the top of a grass blade as you brush against it, so walking in the middle of the trail away from high plants is a good idea. Wearing a hat, a long sleeve shirt tucked into pants, and pants tucked into shoes or socks, also will keep ticks off you, though this is not foolproof as they sometimes can hook onto clothing. A tightly woven cloth provides the best protection, however. Children can pick up a tick that has hitchhiked onto the family dog, so outfit Rover and Queenie with a tick-repelling collar.

After hiking into an area where ticks live, you'll want to examine your children's bodies (as well as your own) for them. Check warm, moist areas of the skin, such as under the arms, the groin and head hair. Wearing light-colored clothing helps make the tiny tick easier to spot.

To get rid of a tick that has bitten your child, drip either disinfectant or rubbing alcohol on the bug, so it will loosen its grip. Grip the tick close to its head, slowly pulling it away from the skin. This hopefully will prevent it from releasing saliva that spreads disease. Rather than kill the tick, keep it in a plastic bag so that medical professionals can analyze it should disease symptoms appear. Next, wash the bite area with soap and water then apply antiseptic.

In the days after leaving the woods, also check for signs of disease from ticks. Look for bulls-eye rings, a sign of a Lyme disease. Other symptoms include a large red rash, joint pain, and flu-like symptoms. Indications of Rocky Mountain spotted fever include headache, fever, severe muscle aches, and a spotty rash first on palms and feet soles that spread, all beginning about two days after the bite.

If any of these symptoms appear, seek medical attention immediately. Fortunately, antibiotics exist to cure most tick-related diseases.

Poison ivy/sumac

Often the greatest danger in the wilds isn't our own clumsiness or foolhardiness but various plants we encounter. The good news is that we mostly have to force the encounter with flora. Touching the leaves of either poison ivy or poison sumac in particular results in an itchy, painful rash. Each plant's sticky resin, which causes the reaction, clings to clothing and hair, so you may not have "touched" a leaf, but once your hand runs against the resin on shirt or jeans, you'll probably get the rash.

To avoid touching these plants, you'll need to be able to identify each one. Remember the "Leaves of three, let it be" rule for poison ivy. Besides groups of three leaflets, poison ivy has shiny green leaves that are red in spring and fall. Poison sumac's leaves are not toothed as are non-poisonous sumac, and in autumn their leaves turn scarlet. Be forewarned that even after leaves fall off, poison oak's stems can carry some of the itchy resin.

By staying on the trail and walking down its middle rather than the edges, you are unlikely to come into contact with this pair of irritating plants. That probably is the best preventative. Poison ivy barrier creams also can be helpful, but they only temporarily block the resin. This lulls you into a false sense of safety, and so you may not bother to watch for poison ivy.

To treat poison ivy/sumac, wash the part of the body that has touched the plant with poison ivy soap and cold water. This will erode the oily resin, so it'll be easier to rinse off. If you don't have any of this special soap, plain soap sometimes will work if used within a half-hour of touching the plant. Apply a poison ivy cream and get medical attention immediately. Wearing gloves, remove any clothing (including shoes) that has touched the plants, washing them and the worn gloves right away.

For more about these topics and many others, pick up this author's "Hikes with Tykes: A Practical Guide to Day Hiking with Kids." You also can find tips online at the author's "Day Hiking Trails" blog. Have fun on the trail!

Index

About the Author

Rob Bignell is a long-time hiker, editor, and author of the popular "Hikes with Tykes," "Headin' to the Cabin," "Hittin' the Trail," and "Best Sights to See" guidebooks and several other titles. He and his son Kieran have been hiking together for the past decade. Rob has served as an infantryman in the Army National Guard and taught middle school students in New Mexico and Wisconsin. His newspaper work has won several national and state journalism awards, from editorial writing to sports reporting. In 2001, The Prescott Journal, which he served as managing editor of, was named Wisconsin's Weekly Newspaper of the Year. Rob and Kieran live in Wisconsin.

CHECK OUT THESE OTHER HIKING BOOKS BY ROB BIGNELL

"Hikes with Tykes" series:
- Hikes with Tykes: A Practical Guide to Day Hiking with Children
- Hikes with Tykes: Games and Activities

"Headin' to the Cabin" series:
- Day Hiking Trails of Northeast Minnesota
- Day Hiking Trails of Northwest Wisconsin

"Hittin' the Trail" series:

National parks
- Best Sights to See at America's National Parks
- Great Smoky Mountain National Park
- Grand Canyon National Park (ebook only)

Minnesota
- Gooseberry Falls State Park

Minnesota/Wisconsin
- Interstate State Park
- St. Croix National Scenic Riverway

Wisconsin
- Barron County
- Bayfield County
- Burnett County (ebook only)
- Chippewa Valley (Eau Claire, Chippewa, Dunn, Pepin counties)
- Crex Meadows Wildlife Area (ebook only)
- Douglas County
- Polk County
- Sawyer County
- Washburn County

GET CONNECTED!

Follow the author to learn about other great trails and for useful hiking tips:

- Blog: *hikeswithtykes.blogspot.com*
- Facebook: *dld.bz/fBq2C*
- Google+: *dld.bz/fBq2s*
- LinkedIn: *linkedin.com/in/robbignell*
- Pinterest: *pinterest.com/rbignell41*
- Twitter: *twitter.com/dayhikingtrails*
- Website: *dayhikingtrails.wordpress.com*

If you enjoyed this book, please take a few moments to write a review of it.
Thank you!